Let's Talk Bilingual!!

Let's Talk Spring Clothes!

¡Hablemos de ropa de primavera!

The Victorian Panda   by/por Amanda Beth Martin

Copyright © 2022 by Amanda Beth Martin

All rights reserved. No part of this book may be reproduced in any form or by any electronic or mechanical means, including information storage and retrieval systems, without express permission in writing from the publisher. For information regarding permission, write to The Victorian Panda, thevictorianpanda@gmail.com.

ISBN 978-1-7356873-6-0 (Paperback Edition)
ISBN 978-1-7356873-7-7 (Ebook Edition)

Let's Talk Bilingual!
Let's Talk Spring Clothes! / ¡Hablemos de ropa de primavera! Amanda Beth Martin

Library of Congress Control Number: 2021904233

First edition: June 2022
Book design by Amanda Beth Martin
Illustrations copyright © by Amanda Beth Martin

Published by The Victorian Panda
www.thevictorianpanda.com
thevictorianpanda@gmail.com

For my Mom,
Thank you for your love, guidance & laughter.

It's spring!

¡Es primavera!

In the spring it starts to get warm and it rains outside.

En primavera empieza a hacer más calor y afuera llueve.

What do we wear in the spring?

¿Qué usamos en primavera?

Let's look in our armoire!

¡Miremos en nuestro ropero!

Rain coat

Un impermeable

Jumpsuit

Un enterizo

Rain boots

Unas botas de lluvia

Tights

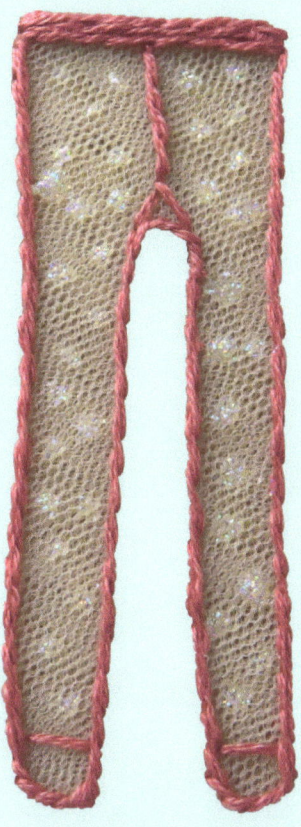

Unas medias

Suspenders

Unos tirantes

Cardigan

Un cárdigan

Umbrella

Un paraguas

Slacks

Unos pantalones

Button up shirt

Una camisa abotonada

Dress shoes

Unos zapatos de vestir

Blouse

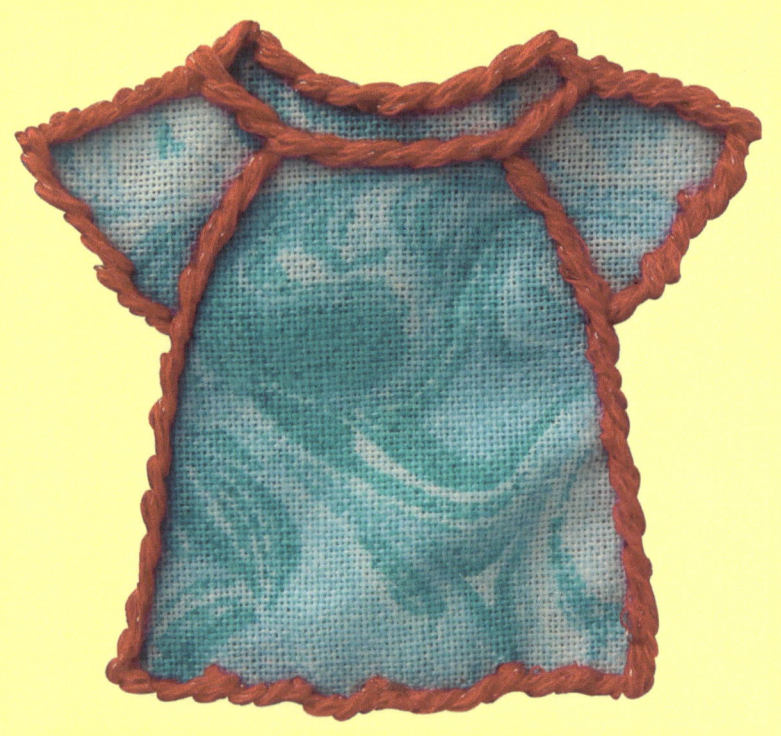

Una blusa

Capris

Unos capris

Jersey

Un jersey

Poncho

Un poncho

Tie

Una corbata

Rain hat

Un gorro de lluvia

What do you like to wear on a rainy spring day?

¿Qué te gusta usar en un día lluvioso de primavera?

www.ingramcontent.com/pod-product-compliance
Lightning Source LLC
Chambersburg PA
CBHW040023130526
44590CB00036B/70